VGM'S CAREER PORTRAITS

FOOD

VGM'S CAREER PORTRAITS

FOOD

Maria Gisler

VGM Career Horizons
a division of NTC/Contemporary Publishing Company
Lincolnwood, Illinois USA

Photo Credits:
Page 1: Copyright © Mark Sherman/Photo Network.
Page 15: Copyright © Michael W. Thomas/Photo Network.
Page 29: Copyright © Bachmann/Photo Network.
Page 43: Copyright © Charlie Yapp/NSP/Photo Network.
Page 57: Copyright © D.L. Baldwin/Photo Network.
Page 71: Copyright © Superstock.
All other photographs courtesy of the author.

Library of Congress Cataloging-in-Publication Data

Gisler, Maria.
    Food / Maria Gisler.
      p.   cm. — (VGM's career portraits)
    Includes bibliographical references (p.)
    Summary: Introduces various food-related jobs, including dietitian, caterer, grocery store manager, and chef, and profiles several people who have been successful in these fields.
    ISBN 0-8442-4381-7
    1. Food service—Vocational guidance—Juvenile literature.
[1. Food service—Vocational guidance. 2. Occupations.] I. Title.
II. Series.
TX911.3.V62G57 1997
647.95'023—dc21   96-48292
                                                          CIP
                                                          AC

Published by VGM Career Horizons,
a division of NTC/Contemporary Publishing Company
4255 West Touhy Avenue
Lincolnwood (Chicago), Illinois 60646-1975, U.S.A.
© 1997 by NTC/Contemporary Publishing Company. All rights reserved.
No part of this book may be reproduced, stored in a retrieval
system, or transmitted in any form or by any means,
electronic, mechanical, photocopying, recording or otherwise,
without the prior permission of NTC/Contemporary Publishing Company.
Manufactured in the United States of America.

Contents

Introduction	ix
Careers in Grocery Stores	1
Let's Meet David Spiller, Administrators Duty Clerk	6
David's Favorite and Least Favorite Things	8
Let's Meet Hayward Cheesebourough, Co-Manager	9
Being Assertive and Getting the Job You Want	11
Success Stories: Barney Kroger and J. Frank Grimes	12
Find Out More	13
Careers in Restaurants	15
Let's Meet Alicia Watson, Service Manager	20
An Unforgettable Job Experience	22
Let's Meet Steve Melanson, Executive Chef	23
Winning a Gold Medal	25
Success Story: McDonald's Restaurants	26
Find Out More	28
Careers in Institutional Foodservice	29
Let's Meet Riley Groover, Foodservice Supervisor	34
Riley's Daily Work Schedule	36
Let's Meet Sandra Fowler, Associate Director	37
What Sandra Likes and Dislikes About Her Job	39
Success Story: The Conveyor Belt	40
Find Out More	41

Careers in Catering — 43
Let's Meet Alice Frigge, Owner of
   a Catering Business — 48
Food and the Party Environment — 50
Let's Meet Monty Watson, Owner of
   a Catering Business — 51
A Challenging Event — 53
Success Stories: Peter O'Grady and
   Denise Vivaldo — 54
Find Out More — 55

Careers in Dietetics — 57
Let's Meet Jill Overton, RD, Certified
   Dietitian — 62
Finding a New Job — 64
Let's Meet Martha Smiley, RD,
   Administration Dietitian — 65
Getting a Head Start on Dietetics
   as a Career Choice — 67
Success Stories: The American Dietetic
   Association and Dr. Ronnie Chernoff — 68
Find Out More — 69

Careers in Teaching about Food — 71
Let's Meet Nancy Ratner, Home
   Economics Teacher — 76
A Look at Nancy's Daily Schedule — 78
Let's Meet Ingrid Friesen, RD, LD,
   Community Resource Educator — 79
Ingrid's First Year on the Job — 81
Success Stories: The California Culinary
   Academy and Cordon Bleu School — 82
Find Out More — 84

Index — 85

There is no love sincerer than the love of food.

> George Bernard Shaw
> *Man and Superman,* 'Tanner'

Dedication

To my family—Mom, Dad, Ann, Mark,
David, and Grandmother—with whom I have shared
so many memorable meals.

Introduction

Food is one of our basic needs. We must have it to survive. Not only does it provide us with the energy for everything we do from walking and talking to working and playing, it also makes us grow and keeps our bodies healthy and strong. Of course, everyone doesn't eat the same thing. What we eat depends greatly on where we live, how much money we have to spend on food, and what we like to eat. The task of providing everyone with the food they eat has made the food industry the largest industry in the world—employing millions of people.

Reading this book will allow you to explore many different careers involving food. Most of the careers will involve direct hands-on contact with food. You'll find out what it is like to have a career associated with grocery stores, restaurants, food education, and institutional foods. You'll also learn what it is like to be a dietitian or caterer. For each of these careers, you will discover what happens on the job, the education and training you need, the pleasures and pressures of the job, the rewards, the pay, the perks, and how to get started now preparing for a future food career. Throughout the book, there will be interviews of individuals actually working right now in food careers.

As you become better acquainted with food careers, you will be able to decide if you have the aptitude, skills, and personality to pursue one of these careers. You will also read stories about prominent people and organizations associated with food.

CAREERS IN GROCERY STORES

The old general store sold food, hardware, pots and pans, medical remedies, and clothing. The modern supermarket concentrates on selling food, but also carries on the tradition of providing a wide array of non-food items and services just like the old general store. Of course, most of the more than 30,000 items in today's stores were never sold in general stores nor did they offer services like video rentals.

> **What it's like to work in a grocery store**

There are more than 125,000 grocery stores in the United States. You may find yourself working in a small neighborhood store or a huge supermarket with many specialty departments. No matter where you work, a grocery store is like a community center because a member of every American household is likely to visit it at least once a week. Because service is a store's main business, you will be working with people who want to help others. You can also expect to work in an environment that is clean and safe.

> **Let's find out what happens on the job**

Your job may consist of sacking groceries, checking out customers, stocking shelves, weighing produce, packaging meat, selling deli or bakery items, or managing a department or even the entire store. Depending on the grocery store, your job might even consist of delivering groceries to customers' homes. Because grocery stores are open long hours, even all night, you can expect to work shifts whether you are a stock clerk, a checker, or a manager. And you can expect to meet and deal with all kinds of people in your job.

Not all jobs associated with grocery stores are within sight of the customers. There are jobs in accounting, advertising, training, engineering, purchasing, law, personnel, security, marketing, real estate, data entry, and trucking to name just a few.

The pleasures and pressures of the job

Here's a job that gives you a chance to serve others. Whatever your job is in a grocery store, you will be making someone's shopping a little easier. At the same time you will have the pleasure of meeting new people in the store every day.

Because customer satisfaction is a major part of the grocery store industry, a job at a large store will usually require working long hours and even holidays. While this may seem like a downside to this job, you will be paid both overtime and holiday pay.

The rewards, the pay, and the perks

Grocery stores provide stable employment because people always need food. Whether you want to work in a grocery store or at a corporate office, many different career paths are available. The path that you choose will set the range of your salary. Starting out as a part-time stock clerk, you should expect to make minimum wage. However, depending on your work experience and the size of the store, you could start slightly above minimum wage. As a full-time clerk, your salary will increase. Expect to be paid hourly until you are in a management position. Most management trainees make from

$18,000 per year to $25,000. Store managers, depending on the volume of the store, can make around $40,000 or more annually. As a full-time worker, you should receive a complete benefits package.

Getting started

Most grocery stores will hire high school students as stock clerks. This job does not require work experience and is where most people start. You can also begin as a checker if you have the appropriate skills. Both of these positions allow you to learn how grocery stores operate and to become acquainted with the many different jobs and departments. This helps you find the appropriate career path. For both store management and corporate positions, a bachelor's degree is becoming more necessary.

Climbing the career ladder

Most managers in the grocery store industry began their careers in either junior high school or high school as stock clerks. The next step up the career ladder for a stock clerk is to become a specialist in a particular area. Or it's possible to become a lead or head stock clerk, which is a supervisory position. This can happen in as little as six months. The next step for checkers is a move to the customer/courtesy booth or to a position as lead checker supervising other checkers.

Working as a specialist in a department like produce or meat can lead to becoming a department manager and to advancing into store management. Assis-tant managers learn on the job how to become store managers. In large chains it is possible to become district managers and even president.

Now decide if a career in the grocery store business is right for you

More than 3 million people work in grocery stores, and it is estimated that there will be openings for at least 600,000 employees in the next 10 years. Do you have the characteristics grocery stores are looking for in their employees?

1. Do you have good people skills?
2. Are you adaptable?
3. Do you have good math skills?
4. Are you willing to learn?
5. Are you energetic and in good shape?

Things you can do to get a head start

The key element on every resume is the experience section. Get a head start on other job seekers by gaining experience through working in a grocery store. While you are in high school, join the Distributive Education Club of America (DECA) to get vocational training in distribution and marketing. And when you are in college, try to get a solid background in basic business skills like math, management, communication, and computer applications.

Let's Meet...

David Spiller
Administrators Duty Clerk

David started working in a grocery store in a small retail food chain when he was in high school and continued working there throughout college.

Tell me how you got started in the grocery store business.

During my junior year in high school, I wanted to get a job. Since I was still in school, the job had to have flexible hours. Luckily, there was a medium-sized, community grocery store just down the street from my home that was hiring. I applied for a position as a service clerk and was hired. I worked as a service clerk for a few years until I was promoted to stock clerk almost two years ago. I am now an Administrators Duty Clerk (ADC).

Did you need any special schooling or training?

I have my undergraduate degree in English and Philosophy; however, the store will provide schooling and training, if you want to have it. Depending on your experience and prior schooling, there is a management training program that you may have to attend and pass before becoming an ADC. Along with strong management skills, you must be a good leader and be able to communicate effectively and deal with both your customers and employees. Depending on the level of promotion, extra training within the company may also be required.

Describe a typical day at work.

No two days are ever the same in this industry. Since I work in a community grocery store, my hours are fairly constant, usually between 50–60 hours a week, depending on volume of sales. I have many management responsibilities and spend most of my time making sure that the aisles I manage are fully stocked and cleaned. Placing orders, contacting suppliers, and training new workers are another part of my job. I also work on the store floor helping customers, taking inventory, stocking the shelves, and even bagging groceries. In this job, you must always be ready to help other coworkers when things get busy. During closing hours, my job entails more management duties. I make sure that each department has completed all daily tasks and is following the correct methods of closing.

Do you think that you are suited to the job?

Since I have a fairly easygoing personality, I think that I work well with both customers and other employees. Most importantly, I have worked hard and have gained the respect of the employees I manage.

David's Favorite and Least Favorite Things

Most Favorite Things about the Job

- Flexible hours allowing him to attend school.
- Customer satisfaction resulting from his hard work.
- Satisfaction of helping a coworker.
- Watching someone he has trained complete tasks successfully.
- Sharing his knowledge of the industry through training new hires.
- Knowing that things move smoothly because of his use of good management skills.
- Not knowing exactly what each day will bring.

Least Favorite Things about the Job

- When he does a job wrong, criticism can come from all sides.
- Not completing scheduled tasks due to other problems arising.
- Trying to motivate employees who do not want to be motivated.
- Seeing a customer unhappy or upset over a mistake that could have been foreseen.
- Having to ask an employee to complete a task for a second time.

Let's Meet...

Hayward Cheesebourough
Co-Manager

Hayward's very first job was in a grocery store, and he has continued to be employed by this large regional supermarket chain ever since.

What first attracted you to a career as a grocery store manager?

As a kid my father had one grocery he preferred above all the other stores. He would always talk about how nice and friendly the workers were at this store. Knowing how much this store appealed to my father, I decided as a junior in high school to try and get my first job there. I started at the store as a service clerk, making very little money. However, after only four weeks and a lot of hard work, I was promoted to produce clerk. I never dreamed that my first job would play such a big role in my career path.

What special skills do you need to be a good co-manager?

Being able to handle stress is one of the most important skills that you need to be a good and effective manager. This includes being able to react quickly to problems. Being able to communicate clearly with employees and customers will also help you to be a more effective manager. You must also be dependable, trustworthy, and responsible.

Describe your work environment.

I work in a high-volume grocery store. Since we service a large community, the work environment is extremely fast paced and can become stressful if not handled correctly.

Do you get to meet a lot of new people on the job?

Yes. Being the co-manager of such a large store, I am constantly helping out customers, hiring and training new employees, and even seeing old friends from school.

What advice would you give young people starting out in the grocery store business?

Be patient. Most people start at a low-level position; however, with hard work and determination, you can move up the ladder. Start with short-term goals and then focus more on the long-term. Keep your eyes open, for there are many good career opportunities within the grocery store business.

If you could start over, would you choose a different career?

No. I would, however, have majored in marketing or management rather than mechanical engineering in college.

Being Assertive and Getting the Job You Want

All of Hayward's hard work, experience, and time with the company paid off when his supervisor promoted him to a co-manager position. He had noticed Hayward's determination and willingness over the years to excel in his career. With this supervisor's recommendation, Hayward was placed in a high-volume store as a co-manager. Even though he worked as a co-manager through college, he decided upon completing college to work on the corporate side. After six years as an engineer, he realized that he missed the management side of the industry and began to direct his career path towards grocery store management. Since Hayward had been a co-manager before and really enjoyed the work, that is where he asked to be placed. Because he had been with the company for so many years, his performance record acted generally as application and interview for the job. However, Hayward believes that if you feel you are being overlooked for a promotion, you must be assertive. Call the corporate office and ask to speak with personnel. Then ask whether they are hiring for a higher-level position and even ask to be placed in a training class. You may want to have a strong resume handy to show you have taken the time to prepare yourself for the position.

Success Stories

Barney Kroger

It was Barney Kroger who first started to put specialty stores together, like bakeries and meat stores, to make grocery shopping what it is today. Barney opened his first grocery store in Cincinnati, Ohio, back in 1883. By 1902, he operated 40 stores and had $1.75 million dollars in annual sales. The stores were known as The Kroger Grocery and Baking Company. A few years later, Barney added another specialty department to the store, the meat department. This was the first time ever meat and groceries were sold under one roof. Over the next 50 years, Kroger grew to become one of the largest grocery store chains. Through extensive market research, Kroger continues to serve their customers by introducing trendsetting specialty shops featuring such items as cheese, deli, and flowers in all of their stores.

J. Frank Grimes

J. Frank Grimes, a Chicago accountant, specialized in auditing books of wholesale grocers. In 1926 he and five associates formed the Independent Grocers Alliance (IGA) to compete with retail chain stores. Their strategy was to create a nationwide network of wholesalers who would work together to bring the independent grocers the power of large-volume buying and lower the cost of goods. IGA has become a global alliance of over 3,600 supermarkets with sales of $16.8 billion annually.

Find Out More

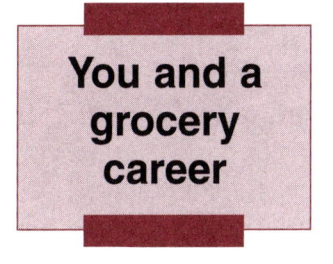

You and a grocery career

This quiz will check to see how much you know about working in a grocery store. If you don't know most of the answers, you need to learn more about the opportunities this career offers.

1. Can you name at least seven jobs that grocery store employees hold?
2. What is the usual entry-level job for most grocery store employees?
3. Why is service so important to the success of a grocery store?
4. Are there great opportunities to get ahead for employees who do well?
5. Do grocery stores offer on-the-job training?
6. Why do grocery store employees need good basic math skills?
7. Why is it so important for grocery store employees to have solid communication skills?
8. Why are jobs in grocery stores considered recession-proof?

> **Find out more about a career in grocery stores**

The best way to get firsthand knowledge about what a career in the grocery business is like is by working during the summer or school year at a local grocery store. There are many ways that you can start your career in the grocery store industry. You can either apply at your local grocery store or contact the corporate office of a chain. You may also want to investigate the possibility of participating in an internship program. For information about careers in grocery stores, contact these sources:

Food Marketing Institute
800 Connecticut Avenue N.W.
Washington, DC 20006

National Grocers Association
1825 Samuel Morse Drive
Reston, VA 20190

CAREERS IN RESTAURANTS

Believe it or not, before the start of the Second World War, many Americans had never eaten in a restaurant. How times have changed! Today, one in three meals is eaten away from the home. With so many people eating out, the restaurant business is the fastest growing business in this country. It employs approximately 5 percent of all the people who work.

What it's like to work in a restaurant

You'll be on your feet most of the time in this job whether you're out front working with customers or in the kitchen preparing food. At meal times the pace will be intense as people crowd into restaurants to be fed. You will have to work quickly and efficiently. As a restaurant worker, you are more likely to be employed part time than full time. Also, you will be expected to work evenings, weekends, and holidays because these are busy times in restaurants.

Let's find out what happens on the job

Restaurants have a strong chain of command. At the top is the manager who has the ultimate responsibility for operating the restaurant. Managers are in charge of selecting items for the menu, setting prices, ordering supplies, dealing with suppliers, supervising all employees, hiring and training new employees, supervising the preparation of food, checking the quality of the food, and such administrative responsibilities as doing the payroll and all the paperwork involved in licensing and following government regulations. Managers often delegate many of their responsibilities to assistant managers. Other employees in restaurants either work with customers as hosts, servers, cashiers, and buspersons or in the kitchen preparing food as chefs, cooks, and kitchen workers.

The pleasures and pressures of the job

Watching people enjoy a meal that you have helped prepare or serve makes all your hard work worthwhile. Hiring bright, ambitious employees and watching their careers develop is a pleasure to those in management. Having a job where rapid advancement is possible is rewarding to entry-level workers.

Working in a restaurant can be hectic during peak dining hours when everyone wants to be served quickly. There is the pressure of taking orders correctly and filling them swiftly and accurately.

The pay and the perks

What you earn in the restaurant industry depends on the part of the country where you live and the type of establishment in which you work. Generally, entry-level employees begin at the minimum wage level or slightly higher. In fast-food restaurants, a low salary for an assistant manager would be $21,000 while a high would be $30,000 excluding bonuses. Fast-food restaurant managers can make as much as $50,000 annually with salary and bonuses, while general managers of restaurants serving liquor can earn a top salary of $60,000. The median annual salary of chefs is $35,000 with executive chefs in renowned restaurants earning $80,000 or more. Most salaried restaurant employees receive a complete benefits package. Part-time workers do not.

Getting started

Education is the key to where you will start in the restaurant industry. Even though a high school diploma is not required for beginning jobs, it is recommended for those planning a career as a cook or chef or in management. Many restaurant employees are able to begin in cook or chef jobs or as management trainees because they have completed training in 2- or 4-year colleges or culinary schools. Also, cooks and chefs can be trained in apprenticeship programs offered by professional culinary institutes, industry associations, and trade unions.

Climbing the career ladder

The restaurant industry is one place where the American dream is possible. You really can climb from an entry-level position to the top. Thirty-four percent of those who now own or operate a restaurant started out as a busperson, dishwasher, or server. After acquiring some basic food handling, preparation, and cooking skills, kitchen workers can advance to assistant cook or short-order cook. It will, however, take many more years of training and experience for them to become chefs in fine restaurants. Entry-level workers often advance to assistant manager or management trainee. For both managers and chefs, willingness to relocate often is essential for advancement to positions with greater responsibility.

Now decide if working in a restaurant is right for you

Your personal qualities are more important in the restaurant business than in almost any other. Do you have what it takes?
"I have _____."
- self-discipline
- initiative
- good leadership skills
- the ability to communicate with others
- good listening skills
- good problem-solving techniques
- a genuine liking and understanding of people
- solid organizational skills
- an appreciation of food
- good health and stamina
- a clean and neat appearance
- a sense of humor
- an ability to handle pressure
- a sense of fairness

Things you can do to get a head start

Find a local restaurant and apply for a part-time job. Do not limit yourself to one type of restaurant, but try both fast-food and full-service restaurants. This will allow you to see the difference between the two and get a better feel for the type of restaurant in which you may want to work.

Let's Meet...

Alicia Watson
Service Manager

Alicia is the service manager of a large sit-down restaurant that is part of a national chain. She wanted to work in management in order to grow more as a person.

What do you especially enjoy about working as a manager?

I enjoy the sense of accomplishment when the day has gone well. I like the fast-paced environment and the need to think on my feet and improvise in a pinch. It's also rewarding to be able to help employees grow and advance in their careers.

Did you need any special schooling or training?

I've attended lots of seminars and classes throughout my career. The most enjoyable experience was a two-week training program in Orlando, Florida where I learned everything from waiting and cooking to managing a restaurant.

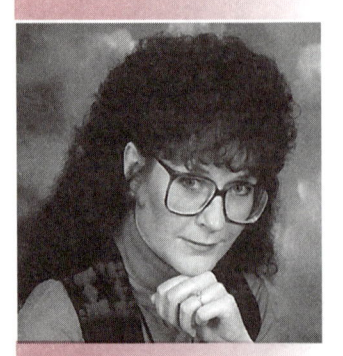

What special skills do you need to be a good manager?

To be a good restaurant manager, you have to be able to deal well with people whether they are employees or guests. You must have at least a slight knowledge of foods. Math and organizational skills are also very important.

Is there a lot of competition for jobs in restaurant management?

Not really. It's a very demanding field. There are many long hours and busy days. There always seems to be a problem that needs to be solved. Not everyone can handle the stress of the job.

How did you feel when you got the job?

I was very happy. My previous jobs had not been very fulfilling. I was starting to doubt my abilities when I got the job; however, now I have surpassed my own expectations. I feel the possibilities for advancement are endless.

What do you see yourself doing five years from now?

My long-term goal is to own a restaurant. I've planned out every detail, right down to the curtains. I will probably stay at my current job for at least five more years. Right now I am a service manager and would like to work up to being a general manager—even higher.

Describe your happiest moments on the job.

It always makes me feel good to hear employees say how glad they are to have me around. It also makes me happy to have positive feedback from other managers and upper management. One of the best feelings is when a guest compliments you for your efforts.

An Unforgettable Job Experience

While working as a manager at a buffet-style steak house, Alicia had the pleasure of meeting the Moscow Boys Choir. About 75 young men under the age of 15, plus their chaperones, stopped by the restaurant for lunch while on tour. These young men spoke little to no English. Alicia assisted the servers in taking care of the group. A lot of their communication involved pointing and using single words: More? Pepsi? Please? and Thank you. It was wonderful watching the boys' delight at an "all you can eat" buffet, complete with ice cream. That is something that they had never experienced before in their own country. Everyone left satisfied and full. The chaperones who were also from Moscow expressed their thanks and told Alicia how much they appreciated the staff's patience, kindness, and friendliness. It was great for Alicia and her staff to have the chance to show goodwill to people from another country.

Careers in Restaurants

Let's Meet...

Steve Melanson
Executive Chef

Steve is the executive chef at a hotel that is part of a large chain. Working as a chef allows him to be creative with the flavors of foods.

What first attracted you to a career as a chef?

I started working as a cook part time while beginning a career as a police officer. After a year I saw that I had more opportunities to earn a higher salary as a chef. That is when I really decided to begin my career as a chef.

Did you need any special schooling or training?

I worked as a sous (assistant) chef for two years under a European chef. That is where I learned the majority of my skills.

Describe a typical day at work.

There really is no typical day for me. Sometimes I come into work extremely early, and sometimes I work only late hours. It really depends on the size of the restaurant or hotel where you work. You may also be given different assignments to work on. Every day brings new challenges.

What special skills do you need to be a good chef?

You need to have some artistic and creative ability. Each plate, buffet, and party that you prepare must be art. It is also important to have strong interpersonal skills. You must be able to manage and deal effectively with other people.

What do you like most about your job?

While the opportunity to make good money is definitely a plus in my job, the ability to use my artistic and creative talents is an important part of my job.

What do you like least about your job?

The long hours. I often have to work weekends, nights, and holidays.

Is there a lot of competition for jobs as a chef?

No. There are definitely a lot more jobs than there are qualified workers. The restaurant business, especially for a chef, has an excellent future job outlook.

What advice would you give young people starting out as a chef?

It is important that you get a broad base of experience. The foodservice industry is one of the few in which you can try different jobs while you are still in school.

Winning a Gold Medal

As he began his career as a chef, Steve also began to compete in various culinary competitions. The very first competition that he ever competed in was the Culinary Salons Competition. In order to compete in the competition, he had to read and become familiar with all the rules of the competition, which for culinary competitions were extremely complicated. Steve entered an 84-pound block of Emmentaler, which is a type of Swiss cheese, carved like the European sun on the shield of Henry XIV. The carving took him over 200 hours to do, and he did all of it at night after work. While it was a lot of hard work, it all paid off when he won the gold medal. Over the next few years, he went on to win 25 more medals in different culinary competitions.

Success Story

The two McDonald brothers, Dick and Mac, opened their first McDonald's restaurant in San Bernardino, California in 1948. The two brought assembly-line production to the fast-food industry. Each worker in their restaurant had a specific task such as grilling, frying, or making shakes. Furthermore, each task was broken down into detailed steps that were always to be followed. Soon people were flocking to their restaurant and were astounded by how fast-food was prepared. This restaurant only had self-service windows; there were no seats inside for customers.

By the early 1950s, there was so much interest in their methods and equipment that the brothers began to sell franchises. They weren't too interested in franchising nor very successful at it. In 1954, Ray Kroc became their second franchising agent, and it is Ray who started McDonald's on its way to becoming a giant in the fast-food industry. Within five years, McDonald's opened its 100th restaurant, and then just one year later the 200th restaurant was opened. In 1961, Ray bought out the McDonald brothers, and in 1965, the first public stock offering occurred. In 1967, McDonald's went international, and just one year later there were 1,000 stores. By 1988, McDonald's had more than 10,000 stores, and the chain keeps growing throughout the world. When you travel you don't have to worry about not finding a Big Mac, for there are McDonald's restaurants even as far away as Russia, China, Japan, and Brazil.

While the number of restaurants was expanding dramatically, many innovations were also taking place inside. In 1963, Filet-O-Fish was the first item added to the original restaurant menu. Then in 1967, indoor seating was introduced. And in 1968, the Big Mac first appeared, while Egg McMuffin came on the scene in 1973. It wasn't until 1975 that the first drive-thru was inaugurated, and home delivery started as recently as 1993.

The McDonald's restaurant chain has had a tremendous impact on the people in the United States. According to *Time* magazine, many people think of the company as a public institution. Children of all ages love the McDonald's characters. In fact, young children often recognize Ronald McDonald better than any of the other characters that are seen on Saturday morning TV shows.

Find Out More

Find out more about working in a restaurant

The best way to learn about a career in the restaurant business is by working in a restaurant and talking to the other employees. You can also contact the following organizations for career information:

The Educational Foundation of
  the National Restaurant
  Association
250 South Wacker Drive, Suite
  1400
Chicago, IL 60606

American Culinary Federation
Educational Institute
P.O. Box 3466
St. Augustine, FL 32084

Culinary Institute of America
P.O. Box 53
Hyde Park, NY 12538

You can learn more about what is happening in the restaurant business and where jobs are by reading the following publications:

Restaurants & Institutions
Nation's Restaurant News
Restaurants USA

CAREERS IN INSTITUTIONAL FOODSERVICE

When you think of people eating outside of their homes, do you just see them eating meals at fast-food restaurants, family-style restaurants, cafeterias, theme restaurants, or white tablecloth places? If so, you have neglected to think of the millions of people who eat at institutions such as schools and hospitals every day. Behind all the food served in these places, there are jobs for people to plan, prepare, and serve millions of meals.

What it's like to be in institutional foodservice

You have a huge choice of places to work—schools, colleges, hospitals, nursing homes, the armed forces, jails, and company restaurants and cafeterias. Or you might work at a large kitchen facility preparing meals for airlines, schools, or box lunches. You'll be able to find traditional restaurant jobs such as busperson, server, chef, cook, and kitchen worker. There are also jobs for dietitians and even conveyor belt workers. In most institutional foodservice facilities, the manager is assisted by one or more assistant managers who will monitor the service of the dining room, cafeteria line, or production line. There will also be an executive cook in charge of the operation of the kitchen.

Let's find out what happens on the job

Besides supervising the preparation and serving of meals, managers select and price menu items, order supplies, deal with suppliers, hire and fire employees, and investigate and resolve customers' complaints. Time is also spent handling administrative responsibilities. This can include keeping accurate records of employee hours, preparing the payroll and work schedule, and doing paperwork to comply with licensing laws and reporting requirements of tax, wage and hour, unemployment compensation, and Social Security laws.

In large facilities, much administrative work will be delegated to assistants.

The pleasures and pressures of the job

As a manager or employee in institutional foodservice, you may work more conventional hours than most restaurant employees. Office and factory cafeterias are often open only on weekdays for breakfast and lunch, and public schools are closed in the summer and for holidays. On the other hand, there is almost a constant need for food in hospitals, jails, and the armed services. This means serving food seven days a week and on holidays and working different shifts. Because institutional foodservice facilities often offer a new menu each day, you may have both the challenge and pressure of selecting new items on a daily basis.

The pay and the perks

Expect salaries to vary greatly between foodservice institutions. Your job also plays a major role in determining your salary. As an entry-level employee, expect to make minimum wage or slightly better depending on your experience and the size of the institution. You may even receive free meals and uniforms. Your salary will increase as you move up the career ladder; managers of large institutional foodservice facilities can earn more than

$45,000 a year. There is also the possibility of bonuses and incentive payments. One solid advantage of working full time for large foodservice facilities is the possibility of having excellent benefits packages.

Getting started

It is easy to get started within the foodservice department of an institution. Companies, public schools, universities, hospitals, and jails are always looking for good people to fill entry-level positions. These jobs do not typically require experience; however, any restaurant experience will be beneficial. If you are looking for a position in management, trainees are usually hired from among the graduates of 2-year and 4-year college programs. Preference is given to graduates with degrees in restaurant and institutional foodservice management.

Climbing the career ladder

Opportunities for advancement are excellent in institutional foodservice. Besides being selected as a management trainee, many entry-level employees who have demonstrated their potential for handling increased responsibility can become assistant managers or management trainees. However, you must be aggressive and work hard before being considered for the management path.

Although it is not required for advancement, earning the designation of certified Foodservice Management Professional (FMP) provides recognition of professional competence, especially if most of your skills were largely acquired on the job. The Educational Foundation of the National Restaurant Association awards this designation to managers who have met certain requirements.

Now decide if a career in institutional foodservice is right for you

You like to work with food but you may not want to work in a restaurant. You like to help others and can envision yourself preparing or serving meals that fit the very special needs of occupants of nursing homes or patients at hospitals. You like the challenge of selecting menus, preparing, and/or packaging food for airlines or special events. If this description begins to describe you, then institutional foodservice may be the career path for you.

Things you can do to get a head start

First of all, find out what it is like to work in institutional foodservice. Volunteer or get a job serving meals or working in the kitchen of a nursing home or hospital while you are in high school. Another option is working in your school cafeteria.

Let's Meet...

Riley Groover
Foodservice Supervisor

Riley has been a cook and a chef and is now in charge of all foodservice on the early morning shift at a prison.

Is a career in foodservice something you always dreamed of?

No. In high school I trained in the building construction trade. It was not until later that I became interested in foodservices after I began to find the construction business unstable.

Did you need any special schooling or training?

I believe that special schooling increases your ability to perform your job. I have an associate degree in Hotel/Motel Management, Culinary Arts, from Ivy Tech and a Dietary Manager degree from Ball State University. With this solid background, I feel that I am better able to perform my duties as a foodservice supervisor.

How did you know you would enjoy working as a foodservice supervisor?

After completing Ivy Tech, where I trained to become a chef in the foodservice industry, I had the opportunity to work as a supervisor of kitchen employees and discovered that I enjoyed being a supervisor.

Do you use the knowledge/skills you learned in school on the job?

Yes. Using the cooking skills that I acquired in school helps me to coordinate the daily preparation of meals to be served. With my management skills I am able to work with my kitchen workers and guide them through their daily tasks.

What do you see yourself doing in the next five years?

I plan to continue taking advantage of all the educational opportunities that I can. They will help me to continue moving up the institutional foodservice ladder. I also feel that new experiences will help me do a better job in any future positions.

What is your next career move likely to be?

I would like to move into the position of foodservice director. This will enable me to set up more training programs and help motivate the employees.

What advice would you give young people starting out in institutional foodservices?

I would say good organizational skills are some of the best skills you can acquire. Also, it is important to learn and train on all aspects of the job.

Riley's Daily Work Schedule

My main job is to supervise the employees on my staff.

1:45 am	Arrive at work.
1:50 am	Receive briefing from bakery shift.
2:00 am	Do paperwork.
2:20 am	Brief the cook so he can instruct the other employees on how much food to prepare for breakfast and lunch.
3:00 am	Check preparation and cooking of the food. Also, check other areas of the kitchen that might need to be cleaned again.
4:00 am	Check the number of employees coming to work to make sure that all the areas have enough workers.
4:10 am	Supervise the feeding of breakfast to kitchen workers.
4:30 am	Supervise the feeding of breakfast to all of the people within the institution.
6:00 am	Supervise the cleaning of areas and begin the preparation of lunch. Also, continue with paperwork and make sure the shift runs smoothly.
9:00 am	Supervise the kitchen workers' lunch.
9:30 am	Supervise lunch for the people within the institution.
9:50 am	Brief the supervisor who will run the next shift on any changes for lunch and any problems that might affect the next shift.

Careers in Institutional Foodservice

Let's Meet...

Sandra Fowler
Associate Director

Sandra works in foodservice at a very large midwestern university and enjoys teaching young employees about this career.

What first attracted you to a career in institutional foods?

I have always enjoyed cooking, even as a child. My mother and I used to experiment with recipes. To expand my knowledge of foods, I decided to take a few science courses along with a home economics course in high school.

Describe a typical day at work.

There is no standard or typical day for me. Every day I am faced with new challenges, which is what makes my job so exciting. While I spend a lot of my day talking with the supervisors of each dormitory, I also deal with students and faculty members. Hiring new employees and maintaining a good solid staff is also a big part of my job. I spend a lot of my time in meetings with the dietitian, chef, and facility supervisors discussing new ways of improving our current menu selection. Planning, organizing, and implementing new ideas is also a major part of my job.

What do you like most about your job?

I really enjoy the interaction that I have with the employees on my staff. I like having the opportunity to offer encouragement to young employees on a day-to-day basis. Researching new recipes with both the dietitian and chef for new events, programs, or just the daily menu is also an exciting part of my job.

What is the most difficult part of your job?

For me, an extremely difficult part of the job is having to discipline members of the staff. This can include having to speak to an employee about bad work habits or dealing with an employee's negative attitude. I also do not like having to deny a promotion to an employee.

What advice would you give young people starting out in institutional foodservice?

Get as much hands-on training as you can. Try to volunteer at a hospital, school, or company. Any job that you can get that allows you to work within a food environment will help you in the future. Also, try to take some food chemistry, science, and math courses while in school. That way you can see if you are interested in these subjects.

What Sandra Likes and Dislikes About Her Job

Favorite Aspects of Her Job

- The sheer challenge of a hectic, chaotic schedule
- Working with the chef
- Developing new training programs for the workers
- Networking with her colleagues in other industries
- Keeping abreast of an ever-changing work environment

Her Greatest Challenges

- Attending meetings that are not productive
- Maintenance problems
- Processing reports and inventories
- Investigating grievances

Success Story

The Conveyer Belt

While conveyor belts have been around for centuries, they did not become popular in industrial businesses until the late 1800s. Conveyor belts are mechanical devices that move materials from one location to another. Within the foodservice industry, the conveyor belt allows food items to be prepared, packaged, and/or labeled quickly. Institutional foodservice companies, for example, that have contracts to provide food for airlines use conveyor belts in the preparation of thousands of meals each day. Both fast-food restaurants and foodservice institutions use conveyor belts to cook items like hamburgers. The raw burger is placed on the belt and then travels over a grill until it reaches the end of the line cooked to just the right degree of doneness.

Conveyor belts are widely used in food processing plants where they advance food from raw product to canned or frozen food as the food goes through such steps as washing, sorting, adding ingredients, and cooking. One of the real benefits of conveyor belts is how they have increased the speed of the last phase of the process when the products are packaged and labeled. The mass production needed within the foodservice industry would be impossible without conveyor belts.

Find Out More

You and institutional foodservice

Take this quiz to see if you share many of the characteristics of successful institutional foodservice supervisors or managers.

Personality
- I am a positive person.
- I like to work with many people.
- I can motivate others.
- I can handle pressure and a fast-paced job.
- I am self-disciplined.

Job Skills
- I can easily communicate what has to be done to other people.
- I can act effectively as a leader.
- I can find effective solutions to problems.
- I can take the initiative in getting things done.
- I can recognize where problems may arise before anything occurs.
- I am always eager to learn more about what I am doing.

> **Find out more about a career in institutional foodservice**

Firsthand work experience in an institutional foodservice facility is the best way to find out if you are truly interested in this type of career. However, you can learn more about all the options this career presents from the following organizations:

Food Service Industry Training
    Program and Facilities
U.S. Department of Health,
    Education, and Welfare
Government Printing Office
Washington, DC 20000

Food Preparation and
    Management
Institutions Books
1801 Prairie Avenue
Chicago, IL 60619

Safety, Sanitation, and Food
    Protection
National Restaurant Association
1530 North Shore Drive
Chicago, IL 60610

CAREERS IN CATERING

Busy households! Party plans! Dinner for the boss! A wedding reception! Lunch in the executive dining room! Birthday parties! Celebrations on yachts! In today's hectic world, it is the caterer who steps in and handles the event from food to mood for the hosts, whether they are individuals, organizations, businesses, or clubs.

What it's like to be a caterer

You are an accomplished cook and menu planner. You also know how to run a business and find new customers. Your workplace may be your own home, an office, a restaurant, a hotel, or even a mobile catering truck. And you will own or rent a considerable amount of equipment from tablecloths to candelabras to vans. Your major job is to plan, prepare, and serve meals for large and small affairs. However, it often extends to setting tables, arranging flowers, hiring musicians, and selecting decorations to set the occasion's mood.

Let's find out what happens on the job

A caterer usually works side by side with the customer to develop a plan for the event within an agreed upon budget. This includes selecting a menu, setting the exact time of the event, and deciding exactly what services the caterer will provide. A contract needs to be signed. A checklist is necessary so no detail is overlooked. Schedules have to be made stating when each food item will be prepared and when it will be served. Additionally, it may be necessary to hire staff beyond yourself and your usual employees. Once an event starts you are a ringmaster coordinating everything that happens. After the event is over, you do your bookkeeping, pay your bills, and evaluate how the event went. Then it is time to plan the next event.

The pleasures and pressures of the job

Being a caterer, you will have the opportunity to meet and work with many new and interesting people. You might have the chance to cater a party for a rock star or a civic leader. Also, you will work closely with the owners of speciality shops such as flower shops and art galleries. And you may cater parties in exotic locales from balloons to Hollywood sound stages.

There are, however, downsides to catering. Clients frequently want to change plans at the last minute. Extra guests may arrive. The florist may be late. A server may not show up. There is always the pressure of making each event a perfect one.

The rewards, the pay, and the perks

One of the rewards of being a caterer is being your own boss. It is also rewarding to be paid for something you like to do—plan parties. The demand for caterers is expected to increase. On the other hand, the number of skilled people wanting to becoming caterers is rising. How much you earn depends on many factors: the number and size of events you schedule, the type of events, the area where you live, and your expertise and style as a caterer. Owner-operators of catering firms may make between $18,000 to $80,000 a year, with well-known and popular caterers earning even more. Only caterers employed in hotels and restaurants will have benefit packages.

Getting started

Before you start your own catering business you need experience working in the field. Work for or apprentice to several experienced caterers. This will help you learn how to plan parties as well as to prepare, present, and serve food. Also, you will have contact with rental firms, florists, and musicians that you may want to use when you start your own business. Besides gaining experience on the job, taking classes in catering and food management at vocational schools and community colleges will acquaint you with the fundamentals of food preparation as well as the business side of catering. They will also teach you how to prepare different food items for large groups of people.

Climbing the career ladder

If you start your own catering firm, you will already be at the top of the ladder. Your main goal then will be to increase your client base and the number of events you cater so that your firm will continue to grow. If you work for a large catering firm or a hotel or restaurant catering service, you may start as a server. You could

Careers in Catering

advance to a supervisor position in charge of a buffet line or the employees at catering events. With more experience, training, and schooling you could become manager of the catering service.

Now decide if a career as a caterer is right for you

Caterers love to plan parties. They are spectacular entertainers. At the same time, they love to cook for others. Caterers must be outgoing, friendly people. As a caterer you will have to be able to greet guests, soothe nervous customers, and supervise servers and other workers. You must also be able to work well under pressure. Little things can go wrong, and huge disasters must be averted. You also need to be a great salesperson capable of attracting new clients. Organizational skills are an absolute prerequisite, too.

Things you can do to get a head start

Get a head start on other job seekers by gaining experience through working in some capacity in the foodservice industry. Even a job at a fast-food restaurant will teach you about organizing employees and working under pressure. Do try to improve your cooking skills by taking classes and cooking for family and friends. Begin to develop a repertoire of quality, fail-safe items that you can easily prepare. And read cookbooks constantly to find new dishes to try.

Let's Meet...

Alice Frigge
Owner of a Catering Business

Alice and her husband own and operate a catering business in a large midwestern city.

What first attracted you to a career in catering?

While growing up I often worked in my parents' restaurant. Whether it was after school or during the summer, I would help my parents by doing various jobs around the restaurant. I would often make sandwiches, sodas, and sundaes. However, I also cashiered, cleared tables, and waited on customers. My husband also worked for a restaurant, and I would help him out by cooking or waiting tables. After a few years he began working for a catering business. Once we started to run the business I became a lot more involved in the actual catering.

Describe a typical day.

I usually get to work early in order to get more done before the phones start ringing. I start my day by looking over our schedule. I notice what events are coming up and make sure that we have ordered everything that we need. It is extremely important that we get our orders in early so that preparation on items can be started. Once I have checked on the orders, the phones begin to ring. Most calls are from people asking for price quotes. I prepare these quotes and then either mail or fax them to the customers. Some days I have appointments with customers, salespeople, and/or dealers. During the end of my day, I try to go around and make sure that the business is organized and things are put away.

What do you like most about your job?

I like not being tied down to one thing. I enjoy having the freedom to do new events and meet new people. I also enjoy the flexible hours. I do not work a typical 9 to 5 job, but have the opportunity to work various hours in order to fit my customers' needs and my own.

Do you get to meet a lot of new people on the job?

Yes. I am constantly meeting with new customers. During an event I get to meet the guests of my customers. By attending catering conventions and shows I meet salespeople and other caterers.

What advice would you give young people starting out in catering?

Try to volunteer or work parttime at a catering business. However, at first do not stay with the same type of business. Try to work a little in each area of the business, such as a hotel or restaurant. It is better to get a broad knowledge in the beginning of your career.

Food and The Party Environment

When you think of catering, long tables of food are probably the first things that pop into your mind. While food may seem like the most important item at an event, it is really the environment that sets the stage for a party. It takes a great deal of skill in order to create the image and setting that your customer has chosen. Throughout the initial meeting with your customer to the cleaning up of the event, you and your staff must present yourselves in a professional, courteous, and accommodating way. Good quality food does not only come from the taste, but more importantly the sight. The sight, presentation, and timing of food service is what brings out the best taste of the food.

Careers in Catering

Let's Meet...

Monty Watson
Owner of a Catering Business

Monty's first job involved making pretzels. Since then, he has never had a job that wasn't associated in some way with the food industry.

What first attracted you to a career in catering?

All through high school I worked in a foodservice environment. Actually, it was a bakery that made pretzels for local taverns. It was then that I realized how much I liked working with food.

Did you need any special schooling or training?

Yes, you need some type of background in foods. I received most of my training when I worked as a supervisor for a food company that made all their own food from scratch. As part of my training I spent time working in each department of the company learning how the various types of food in that department were made.

What do you like most about your job?

I like being able to create different flavors and textures with many different types of foods. I also like being able to have time to do things outside my work environment. Catering allows me to be flexible with my time.

Describe your work environment.

Each day brings new and exciting challenges. As the date of each event approaches, things can get busy. You must be able to plan ahead and stay on schedule so that preparation is started. Meals and decorations must be ready on the day of the party. Near the date for an event, you may find yourself working long hours, 10 to 15 hours a day.

Describe one of your happiest moments on the job?

My happiest moments occur when I receive phone calls or letters from customers saying how wonderful they thought an event was. Receiving positive feedback about my work and my employees' work is one of the best parts of my job.

What advice would you give young people starting out in catering?

Try to get a job in a hotel. This will give you a chance to see how various types of food are prepared—breakfast, lunch, dinner, and party food. Through this experience obtain as much knowledge of food as you can. Also, take a few accounting and bookkeeping classes to broaden your business knowledge.

Let's Meet...

Monty Watson
Owner of a Catering Business

Monty's first job involved making pretzels. Since then, he has never had a job that wasn't associated in some way with the food industry.

What first attracted you to a career in catering?

All through high school I worked in a foodservice environment. Actually, it was a bakery that made pretzels for local taverns. It was then that I realized how much I liked working with food.

Did you need any special schooling or training?

Yes, you need some type of background in foods. I received most of my training when I worked as a supervisor for a food company that made all their own food from scratch. As part of my training I spent time working in each department of the company learning how the various types of food in that department were made.

What do you like most about your job?

I like being able to create different flavors and textures with many different types of foods. I also like being able to have time to do things outside my work environment. Catering allows me to be flexible with my time.

Describe your work environment.

Each day brings new and exciting challenges. As the date of each event approaches, things can get busy. You must be able to plan ahead and stay on schedule so that preparation is started. Meals and decorations must be ready on the day of the party. Near the date for an event, you may find yourself working long hours, 10 to 15 hours a day.

Describe one of your happiest moments on the job?

My happiest moments occur when I receive phone calls or letters from customers saying how wonderful they thought an event was. Receiving positive feedback about my work and my employees' work is one of the best parts of my job.

What advice would you give young people starting out in catering?

Try to get a job in a hotel. This will give you a chance to see how various types of food are prepared—breakfast, lunch, dinner, and party food. Through this experience obtain as much knowledge of food as you can. Also, take a few accounting and bookkeeping classes to broaden your business knowledge.

A Challenging Event

Every now and then, Monty has the pleasure of working on an outdoor catering event for a wedding or reception party. He finds these events the most exciting and interesting of all the events he caters. One particular event that he worked on took place under a large tent with a gazebo in the corner. There were about 250 guests at the event. The food was located in one of the wings of the tent, which was shaped like an "L"; the guests, along with a 10-piece band, were located in the other wing. Monty prepared a wonderful buffet for the event, and overall, it was a beautiful affair. The challenge of an outdoor wedding comes from not having a kitchen nearby; all the food must be prepared ahead of time and kept warm while transporting it and setting up the event. The logistics are much harder to plan and carry out than indoor events. While outdoor events are the trickiest to plan for, for Monty they are by far the most rewarding and memorable.

Success Stories

Peter O'Grady

Peter O'Grady has been catering special occasions for major TV and movie stars in the Rocky Mountains of Aspen, Colorado for over 15 years. Peter spends a great deal of his energy and time researching and creating new styles for his already fabulous menus. He enjoys being challenged by new cuisines from around the world; thus, many of his dishes will be Italian and nouveau-American mixes. Peter believes that most of his repeat clients and fully-booked schedule are due partly to the level of cuisine that he prepares. Peter carefully tailors each event to meet his client's needs. In addition to the quality of food, he also feels high quality service is essential. His staff is professional, courteous, and accommodating at all times.

Denise Vivaldo

After a particularly successful party, Denise Vivaldo decided that she should be paid for giving parties. Within a few years after attending a cooking school and apprenticing to several different caterers, she was ready to start her home-based catering business. She began by selling food to special-event planners. Today, more than ten years later, she directs 5 or 6 events a month—from parties for several thousand on a Hollywood sound stage to wedding receptions. She also works with people who want to start their own catering business and has written a book on opening and operating such a business.

Find Out More

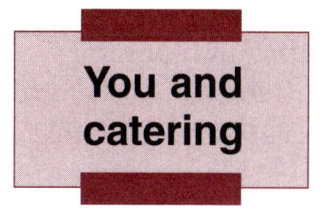

You and catering

Take this quiz to learn what skills you will need to have in order to become a successful caterer.

Cooking Skills
1. I know how to plan meals.
2. I understand the fundamentals of cooking.
3. I can prepare interesting dishes.

Interpersonal Skills
1. I can communicate effectively with people.
2. I can resolve conflicts.
3. I enjoy working with different people.

Creative Skills
1. I can create appealing table and buffet settings.
2. I can use decorations effectively to create a special party atmosphere.

Business Skills
1. I am able to sell myself to others.
2. I know how to keep financial records.
3. I know how to budget.
4. I know how to hire good employees.

Now is a good time to investigate schools that have programs that will improve your cooking skills, teach you how to run a commercial kitchen, and give you extensive practice in planning parties. Many community colleges have degree programs in various aspects of the food industry.

> **Find out more about a career as a caterer**

You can learn even more about catering by reading the following books:

How To Open and Operate A Home-Based Catering Business by Denise Vivaldo, published by The Globe Pequot Press.

Becoming a Chef by Andrew Dornenburg and Karen Page, published by Van Nostrand Reinhold.

This organization has career information about mobile industrial catering trucks (lunch trucks):

Mobile Industrial Caterers Association–International
1240 North Jefferson Street Suite G
Anaheim, CA 92807

CAREERS IN DIETETICS

Dietitians do not only work with people who are sick, but more and more these experts on food and nutrition work with healthy people to help them stay that way. Health, nutrition, and fitness have become a way of life. People are now more aware than ever before of what they eat and are paying close attention to the old saying: "You are what you eat."

What it's like to be a dietitian

You are an expert on food and nutrition. And you work in such places as hospitals, nursing homes, schools, prisons, businesses, government agencies, colleges, food industries, pharmaceutical companies, daycare centers, and healthcare facilities. Like most dietitians, you will probably work a regular 40-hour week, although some do work weekends. More than likely you will be a full-time employee, as only one in five dietitians works part time. Most of your time will be spent in clean, well-lighted, and well-ventilated areas. However, some dietitians do spend time in hot, steamy kitchens. Expect to be on your feet most of the day.

Let's find out what happens on the job

Most dietitians practice in the areas of clinical, community, and management dietetics. As a clinical dietitian you would work with doctors, nurses, and therapists to coordinate medical and nutritional needs. You would also develop and implement nutrition programs. Community dietitians counsel individuals and groups on nutritional practices designed to prevent disease and to promote good health. Management dietitians oversee large-scale meal planning and preparation. Educator dietitians teach foods and nutrition to future doctors, nurses, and dietitians. Research dietitians conduct or direct experiments to answer nutrition questions and find alternative foods.

The pleasures and pressures of the job

Helping people improve their health by eating right is one of the best gifts that one can give. As a dietitian you will show people how to select good foods and how to prepare them correctly so that they can live better. You will help improve the health of overweight patients, diabetics, and critically ill people. You will create tasty and nutritious meals that are appealing to older people in nursing homes and make it enjoyable for them to eat again.

There is the pressure of trying to help ill people. There is also the pressure, in some jobs, of planning meals and directing the entire foodservice for a company, prison, cafeteria, or school.

The pay and the perks

According to the American Dietetic Association, most full-time registered dietitians with 1 to 5 years of experience will make between $25,000 and $35,000. Some may earn as much as $45,000. Dietetic technicians with the same experience typically earn between $20,000 and $30,000. A few will earn close to $40,000. Salaries also vary by educational level, geographical location, and the size of the community. Management and self-employed dietitians typically earn more than clinical and community dietitians. Your salary will increase with experience in the field. You should also expect to receive a complete benefits package.

Getting started

The basic educational requirement to become a dietician is a bachelor's degree with a major in dietetics, foods and nutrition, food service systems management, or a related area. In order to become a registered dietitian with the Commission on Dietetic Registration of the American Dietetic Association (ADA), you must pass a certification exam after the completion of your academic education and supervised practical experience. This experience can be combined with your college work or completed in an ADA-accredited internship or preprofessional practice program.

After you have the needed supervised experience and have passed the test, you are a Registered Dietitian and may use the initials "RD" after your name, showing that you are an expert on food and nutrition. In order to keep your registration current you must attend 75 hours of classes, seminars, or lectures every five years. Graduate programs are available for those interested in research, advanced clinical positions, or public health—where a graduate degree is usually needed.

Climbing the career ladder

Experienced dietitians may advance to the position of assistant, associate, or director of a dietetic department or become self-employed. Some dietitians leave the profession and become sales representatives for equipment or food manufacturers.

Now decide if a career as a dietitian is right for you

A career in dietetics involves working closely with people. Does this appeal to you? Also, you will need to have the initiative to work independently. Ask yourself if you can work well without guidance. Dietitians are problem solvers; are you?

Things you can do to get a head start

If you really think that dietetics is a career possibility for you, start getting ready now. You will study a lot of science in college to get a bachelor's degree in this area. Take biology, chemistry, mathematics, and health in high school. Home economics would be helpful, too, along with sociology, psychology, and business courses.

Let's Meet...

Jill Overton, RD
Certified Dietitian

Jill works in an institute for the blind where she supervises the creation of food and comes up with new meal ideas.

What first attracted you to a career as a dietitian?

I grew up in a home where nutrition was extremely important. My mother did the majority of the cooking and took great care in making sure that we all ate correctly. During my first few years in college I focused mainly on physical therapy; it was not until after a summer as an intern in the nutritional field that I decided it was time to change my major. As a freshman I had taken a nutrition class that I really enjoyed. Luckily, a few of my health classes from my first major overlapped with the requirements for a Bachelor of Science degree in nutrition and dietetics.

Did you need any special schooling or training?

In order to receive an undergraduate degree in nutrition and dietetics, you must complete an internship pertaining to the field. You must also pass an examination to become fully registered with the American Dietetic

Association. In order to keep your registration current you are required to attend 75 hours of classes or seminars every five years.

What special skills do you need to be a good dietitian?

You must be extremely personable. When you are a dietitian at a school and work with other people, you must also be a good listener, communicator, and resource allocator. Being both positive and flexible are also important.

What do you like most about your job?

I like sharing my knowledge of the importance of good nutrition with the children. Seeing the children enjoy their meals is what makes my job so much fun.

Describe your work environment.

I really enjoy the environment in which I work. It is a small industrial food service for a state school. Since we are all here to help teach the children at the school, we work closely together. This closeness encourages all the employees to do their best.

If you could start over, would you choose a different career?

No. I would, however, have liked to learn more about different careers associated with the field, such as kitchen architecture.

Finding a New Job

It was only a few months ago that Jill decided to make a career change after working as a clinical dietitian for 15 years and really enjoying the job. One day while glancing through *The Journal of the American Dietetic Association,* Jill noticed a job opening at a state school for a dietitian. She had no experience in industry foods but thought that the job sounded extremely interesting. As she read the article, Jill noticed that she fit all the requirements for the position: management experience, registered dietitian, and 5–7 years of experience. She called and asked for an application. After completing the application, a job bank reviewed it. Jill received a call a few weeks later saying that her application had been sent to the school and an interview would be arranged. The first interview was within a week. Since it had been awhile since Jill had been on an interview, she brushed up on her interviewing skills. After the interview, she was asked to complete both a list of questions and a personality test. Three weeks later, she received a call from the school asking her back for a second interview. Jill feels extremely lucky to have received a job offer after that interview.

Careers in Dietetics

Let's Meet...

Martha Smiley, RD
Administration Dietitian

Martha is a dietitian at a major midwestern university for all the dormitories and the food service at the union.

What first attracted you to a career in nutrition and dietetics?

As a kid I participated in local 4-H programs. That is where my love for food really began. I enjoyed cooking and experimenting with various foods. My last year in high school I decided to take a home economics class. While that was the only food class that I took in high school, my love for food and nutrition inspired me to earn a bachelor's degree in Hospital Dietetics and Institutional Management.

Describe a typical day at work.

There really is no typical day for me. Most days consist of visiting each dining hall to inspect the hall's food service. At each hall I check to make sure that both the preparation and quality of the food are up to par. I also spend some of my time meeting with our chef. Together we work to standardize recipes for new food items. I am also responsible for providing a nutritional summary of each food item served.

What special skills and knowledge do you need to be a good dietitian?
- Work well with people
- Be a self-motivator
- Have a knowledge of foods and the preparation of foods
- Be creative
- Understand the nutritional value of foods
- Possess good organizational skills

What do you like most about your job?
I really enjoy the planning and writing of new menus. The satisfaction of seeing my plan carried out and completed successfully is something I like about my job.

What is the most difficult part of your job?
It's hard to get a new food item to look exactly like what I imagined in my mind.

What advice would you give young people starting out in a career as a dietitian?
If you are interested in a career as a dietitian, try to work at a hospital or restaurant to expand your knowledge of food. Pay special attention to your science, math, and computer classes in school. Finally, experiment with cooking. Try new recipes, be creative, and have fun.

Getting a Head Start on Dietetics as a Career Choice

Martha believes that any job connected to food or meeting the public will help in future years as a dietitian. She worked summers to earn money for college and finds that she sometimes still refers to those experiences. The summer before she started college she worked in a tomato canning factory. Actually, she was stapling boxes, not peeling or cooking the tomatoes; but Martha still learned the procedure of canning tomatoes.

The next summer she worked in a very busy cafeteria in a large city. Martha was scared to death of the head cook. Consequently, she took as long as possible to finish any task she was assigned, because she didn't want to have to ask the head cook what to do next. Martha advises that's a good thing to remember when a new employee comes to the kitchen and appears to be a slow worker.

The following summer she helped as a diet aide to the dietitians in a large hospital. One of her duties was talking to patients about their likes and dislikes. The most striking thing that she remembers was getting used to the idea that she could go through a door marked "No Admittance, Hospital Personnel Only."

All of these summer experiences helped Martha decide that she really enjoyed working in the foodservice industry and especially dietetics. They gave her a "jump start" on her career.

Success Stories

The American Dietetic Association

With more than 68,000 members, the American Dietetic Association (ADA) is the nation's largest group of nutrition professionals. Their mission is to serve the public through the promotion of optimal nutrition, health, and well-being. The members' vision is to shape the food choices and improve the nutritional status of the public. The ADA plays a key role in influencing such timely issues as food labeling, health care reform, and child nutrition programs. All members of the American Dietetic Association have extensive scientific backgrounds. Each uses his or her knowledge of food, nutrition, biochemistry, physiology, management, and behavioral and social sciences to promote health, prevent disease, and speed recovery from illness.

Dr. Ronnie Chernoff

Dr. Ronnie Chernoff is a leader in the dietetics profession. She served as president of the ADA in 1996–1997 and is currently a professor of Nutrition and Dietetics at the University of Arkansas. Besides holding positions at several other medical centers, Dr. Chernoff is the author and editor of more than 125 publications. She is also a renowned speaker who has delivered more than 350 continuing education lectures during her career.

Find Out More

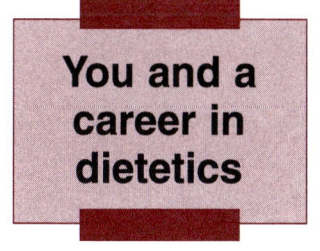

You and a career in dietetics

An important part of succeeding in any career is being able to or wanting to do all the things that are necessary to prepare you for that career. Are you willing to do the following things in order to become a dietitian? Think carefully about your answers. They are important.

1. Are you willing to study biology and chemistry in high school?
2. Are you willing to study home economics?
3. Are you willing to study such sciences as chemistry, microbiology, and physiology in college?
4. Are you willing to earn a bachelor's degree?
5. Are you willing to spend the extra time and effort to become a registered dietitian?
6. Are you willing to take the courses required to keep your ADA certification as a registered dietitian?
7. Are you willing to get a master's degree or even a doctorate to advance in your career?
8. Are you willing to start learning as much as you can about this career?

If you are willing to do everything on this checklist, then dietetics may be the right career choice for you.

Find out more about a career as a dietitian

Dietitians can be found in different settings. Try to find a position as an employee or volunteer in several places so you can begin to learn about the diversity of the jobs that dietitians do. Some of your choices include hospitals, nursing homes, schools, public health clinics, and company cafeterias.

Contact The American Dietetic Association for career information as well as a list of academic programs and scholarship information. You might also look at the organization's journal, which covers the entire profession. Talk to your counselor and ask to see the ADA "Set Your Sights" video for more information.

The American Dietetic Association
216 West Jackson Boulevard
Chicago, IL 60606-6995

CAREERS IN TEACHING ABOUT FOOD

How do you make an omelet? What foods should we be eating every day? Home economics teachers have the answers to these food questions. How do you cater a banquet for 1,000 guests? How can restaurants avoid food spoilage? Instructors at vocational schools and colleges in the area of food preparation, service, and management will have the answers to these questions. Learning about food is important to everyone.

What it's like to be a teacher

If you are teaching about food, you could be a home economics teacher in a middle school or high school. Most public school teachers work the traditional 10-month school year with a 2-month vacation. Part of your time will be spent in the classroom and the other part in the school's food laboratory where the students will prepare food items. You could also be teaching about food in a vocational school or 2- or 4-year college where you would work either part time or full time. There you will probably teach several courses during a semester or quarter. Your students will be taking your classes to prepare for a career in the foodservice industry. You could also be working in a small cooking school—located in your own home, a store, or a school—teaching interested adults and/or children how to cook and serve special dishes.

Let's find out what happens on the job

No matter who you teach, your time will be spent on three tasks. At times, you will be in the front of your class lecturing or leading your students in a discussion. Time will also be spent demonstrating to your students such things as cooking techniques, the proper way to use kitchen utensils, and the preparation of food items. Finally, you will supervise your students as they work in

Careers in Teaching About Food

the food laboratory to create a product. This involves critiquing their work and providing any needed guidance.

The pleasures and pressures of the job

Seeing a student develop new skills and build on existing skills is always gratifying to a teacher. Pleasure is being successful in having 25 students make a great dish that only you could make before. Being able to share a love of food with students is another pleasure, as is the opportunity to work with students who are highly motivated to learn these lifetime skills.

For teachers there is always the need to learn new skills. There is also the pressure of determining the best way to break a task into steps that students can easily accomplish. In addition, teachers must step back and tell students what to do. It's rather like cooking with your hands tied.

The rewards, the pay, and the perks

Beginning teachers in the public schools usually earn somewhere in the range of $24,000–$28,000, depending on their experience and schooling. The average salary for full-time faculty at 4-year colleges is above $45,000. This is higher than the salaries of faculty at 2-year colleges. Full-time teachers at culinary schools can expect first year salaries in the range of $20,000; however, well-known chefs with an international reputation may earn as much as $60,000. All full-time teachers will enjoy a traditional benefits package. One of the perks of teaching is being able to earn extra money through writing books, appearing on television, and giving demonstrations.

Getting started

First of all, if you plan to teach home economics in a middle school or high school, you have two tasks. You need to have a bachelor's degree and to have completed an approved teacher training program with a prescribed number of subject and education credits and supervised student teaching. Teachers at 2-year colleges can obtain positions with only a master's degree; however, 4-year colleges almost always expect full-time faculty members to hold doctoral degrees.

Instructors at culinary schools need to be very skilled in food preparation and/or management. Quite often they will have graduated from a well-known culinary school—perhaps one in Europe—completed apprenticeships with renowned chefs, and gained acclaim through their work in the field. Some will even have written books.

Climbing the career ladder

Home economics teachers in public schools can become department chairs. At the 4-year college level, most teachers enter as instructors or assistant professors. The next step is associate professor followed by the top step of professor. Teachers at 2-year colleges often begin as part-time instructors before getting full-time status.

Now decide if a career as a teacher is right for you

Demand is skyrocketing for skilled people in the foodservices industry. More teachers will be needed, especially to train cooks and chefs and to teach management skills. Should you be one of those teachers? Think about how you would complete this statement: "I would like to have a job that involves _____."

- working with food in some way
- teaching basic cooking skills
- teaching restaurant management
- working in a 2- or 4-year college
- working in a culinary school
- working part time
- working full time

After you know your job preferences, you are ready to explore exactly which teaching career is best for you.

Let's Meet...

Nancy Ratner
Home Economics Teacher

Nancy is a high school teacher who believes teaching is entirely a team concept. In the classroom you are the team leader and out of the classroom you are a staff player.

Is a career in teaching something you always dreamed of?

I never really considered becoming a teacher until I moved to New York. My dad had thought it was a good idea for a woman in college to get a teaching degree so that she could always get a job. That is the only reason I completed the additional requirements in education and followed through with student teaching.

How did you know you would enjoy working as a teacher?

I did not know I would enjoy teaching until I actually tried it. I then found I related quite well with young adults.

Did you need any special schooling or training?

A 4-year college degree is required. This includes major and minor fields of study, required basic education courses, and a semester of student teaching. Most teachers go on to graduate school to earn a master's degree.

What do you like most about your job?

The students! I really enjoy the classroom environment. I interact with approximately 120 students a day in various classes. I often think I learn as much from them as they learn from me.

Do you think you are suited to the job?

Yes, I have proven over the past 19 years that I am well suited to the job of teaching. My students generally do well, and I have very few discipline problems in the classroom.

Describe one of your happiest moments on the job.

Several years ago I was named "Teacher of the Year" by my fellow high school teachers. This was a great compliment from my peers.

What do you like least about your job?

1. Parents who are not interested in their children.
2. Interference from non-educators who rarely deal with children.
3. Pointless, meaningless paperwork.
4. Unproductive staff meetings.

What advice would you give young people starting out in teaching?

Make sure you truly care about children. Have a good sense of humor and confidence in yourself. More importantly, really believe in what you are doing.

A Look at Nancy's Daily Schedule

On a typical day, Nancy arrives at work at 7:00 am. The first thing that she does is sign in at the main office. From 7:00 to 7:15, she sets up the activities that she has planned for first period. While the students begin arriving at 7:15, classes don't actually begin until 7:30. From 7:15 to 7:30, students begin to enter the classroom and get ready for the start of class. Between 7:30 in the morning and 2:30 in the afternoon, Nancy has five 45-minute classes, one preparation period, one lunch supervision period, and one lunch period. During her lunch supervision time, she walks around the cafeteria and grounds where students are allowed during lunchtime, making sure that everything is going smoothly. Classroom activities vary on a daily basis. Her preparation period allows her to get ready for these different activities so that she doesn't have to take a lot of time during the 45-minute class for setting up activities. Some days Nancy is also involved in after-school meetings and workshops.

Let's Meet...

Ingrid Friesen, RD, LD
Community Resource Educator

Ingrid works at a large hospital and teaches people the importance of eating healthy and shows them how to change their eating habits.

What first attracted you to a career in teaching?

I really did not know exactly what I wanted to do when I began college. I knew that I was not interested in becoming a doctor or nurse, but I had really enjoyed my science classes in high school. I also enjoyed working with foods and people. So I decided to get my bachelor's degree in food, nutrition, and dietetic studies.

Describe a typical day at work.

Since I have the opportunity to engage in so many different activities, I do not really have a typical day. The majority of my work is for the community; therefore, I gear most of my education classes to fit these needs. I often meet with patients one on one and also put together presentations and provide newspaper columnists with new information.

What special skills do you need to be a good teacher?

It is extremely important that you have the ability to communicate effectively with people. You must also be able to adapt to each individual's learning capabilities. Being creative will help you come up with new activities that will enhance your students' learning.

What do you like most about your job?

I find my job very rewarding. It is a wonderful feeling to know that you are educating people to improve their health. I enjoy sharing my love of food with others in fun, creative programs.

How did you feel when you got your first promotion/raise?

I received my first raise after one year on the job. It felt good to know that my hard work was being recognized.

What is your next career move likely to be?

I will probably continue with my education. I would like to get my master's degree in either counseling or education. I would also like to broaden my view of health service.

What advice would you give young people starting out in teaching?

Do not be afraid of trying new things; this is the best way to learn. Also, try to get as much experience as you can. Volunteering is an excellent way to see if you would enjoy a career as a health educator.

Ingrid's First Year on the Job

Ingrid really didn't have a set job description when she began her job at the hospital. She knew that she was hired to develop a nutritional/health and wellness program to fit the needs of both the hospital and community. After looking at the most important needs of the people, Ingrid decided to create a healthy eating series. The series that she created is 7 weeks long and based on the Food Guide Pyramid. Each weekday is filled with improving and gaining knowledge of one part of the pyramid. A big part of the day is lunchtime. This is when a special meal is served, depending on the week, and a discussion of the food takes place. Ingrid helps the students learn the importance of the type of food that they are eating and what they should look for when buying the food. Finally, on the last day each student makes up a meal menu and brings in his or her own lunch. The group then discusses what food items were brought in the brown bags.

Success Stories

The California Culinary Academy

The California Culinary Academy is one of the premier culinary arts institutions in the United States. It is located in San Francisco, California, which is considered by many as the culinary capital of the United States because of its 3,500 restaurants and diverse ethnic influences. The Academy was founded in 1977 as a professional training school for aspiring chefs and is housed in the historic California Hall, which was constructed in 1912 as a social club and theater. The building features an 80-foot-high barrel vaulted ceiling, iridescent skylights, and terrazzo and marble floors. It makes an impressive setting for the school. Besides classrooms and kitchen facilities for practical training, the school has 3 full-service, student-run restaurants seating more than 700 customers for lunch and dinner 5 days per week. It also operates a small retail shop which sells products made in several of the classes.

The school accommodates approximately 765 students in its 2 professional education programs: the 16-month Culinary Arts Program and a 30-week certificate program in baking and pastry arts. The comprehensive and intensive 16-month program leads to an associate of occupational studies degree. Students attend hands-on cooking classes and receive instruction in food and beverage management. Graduates are qualified for careers in cooking, dining room service, restaurant management, and ownership. Participants in the professional baking and pastry program master the baking procedures, techniques, skills, and presentation that are necessary to succeed in this field. Graduates receive an accredited certificate in baking and pastry arts. The school also has a weekend professional skills program for those who are working and interested in a career in the culinary arts.

The school reached out to all cooking aficionados through its television series, *Cooking at the Academy*. The school also receives professional input through its Educational Advisory Committee which includes such well-known figures as Julia Child, Robert Mondavi, and Martin Yan.

Cordon Bleu School

The Cordon Bleu in Italy is a well-known European cooking school. Cooks from all over the world travel to Rome, Italy to learn from the two teachers—and founders—of the school: Cristina Blasi and Gabriella Mazi. The Cordon Bleu was established in 1966 to teach both professional and amateur cooking. The school offers a wide range of activities in the cooking area. While attending the school, students have the opportunity to use all of the facilities provided: a well equipped kitchen laboratory, a library, and a wine and food tasting area. All classes are taught in Italian, English, and French. During the spring, summer, and fall semesters, classes concentrate generally on Italian cooking and Italian regional cooking. Other classes that are taught at the school are: Basic Cooking, Christmas Specialities, Fish and Seafood, Chocolate, and Typical Italian Fried Donuts.

Find Out More

Find out more about teaching

One of the best way to find out more about a career as a teacher is to follow a home economics or culinary arts teacher around for a day. By "job shadowing," you can see exactly what a career in that field is like. Information on certification for public school systems is available from state Departments of Education. You can also contact the following organizations to answer your questions on teaching:

American Federation of Teachers
555 New Jersey Avenue N.W.
Washington, DC 20001

National Education Association
1201 16th Street N.W.
Washington, DC 20036

You can learn more about educational programs from the following books:

A Guide to College Programs in Hospitality & Tourism, published by John Wiley & Sons, Inc., New York.

The Guide to Cooking Schools–1996, published by ShawGuides, Coral Gables, Florida.

Directory of Institutional Members, published by the International Association of Cooking Professionals, Washington, DC.

INDEX

Administration dietitian profile, 65–67
Administrators duty clerk (ADC) profile, 6–8
American Culinary Federation, 28
American Dietetic Association (ADA), 59, 60, 62–63, 68, 70
  profile, 68
American Federation of Teachers, 84
Apprenticeship, 18, 46, 74
Artistic and creative talent, 24
Associate degree, 34, 82. *See also* 2-year college program
Associate director profile, 37–39

Bachelor's degree, 4, 6, 10, 32, 34, 60, 62, 65, 69, 76
  teacher training program, 74
Becoming a Chef, 56
Blasi, Cristina, 83
Busperson, 16, 18, 30

California Culinary Academy, 82–83
Cashier, 16
Catering, 43–56
Catering business owner profile, 48–49, 51–53
Certificate program, 82
Certification, 60, 84
Certified dietitian profile, 62–64
Checker, 4
Cheesebourough, Hayward, 9–11
Chef, 16, 17, 30
  skills of, 24
  profile of, 23–25
Chernoff, Ronnie, Dr., 68
Child, Julia, 83
Clerk, 3
Clinical dietetics, 58
Co-manager profile, 9–11
College teaching, 72
Commission on Dietetic Registration of the ADA, 60
Communication skills, 9–10
Community college, 46, 56. *See also* 2-year degree program
Community dietetics, 58
Community resource educator profile, 79–81

Competition, 21, 24
Computer expertise, 5
Conveyor belt history, 40
Cook, 16, 18, 30
Cooking at the Academy, 83
Cordon Bleu, 83
Culinary Arts Program, 82
Culinary Institute of America, 28
Culinary Salons Competition, 25
Culinary school, 18, 74
  teaching, 72

Department chair, 75
Department of Education (state), 84
Dietetics career, 57–70
Dietitian profile, 62–64
Directory of Institutional Members, 84
Dishwasher, 18
Doctoral degree, 60–61, 74
Dornenburg, Andrew, 56

Education and training, 6–7, 18, 20, 34, 60, 62–63
Educational Foundation of the National Restaurant Assoc., 28, 33
Educator dietitian, 58
Executive chef profile, 23–25

Fast-food restaurant/industry, 17, 19, 26, 40
Food Marketing Institute, 14
Food Preparation and Management, 42
Food Service Industry Training, 42
Foodservice Management Professional (FMP) certification, 33
Foodservice supervisor profile, 34–36
Fowler, Sandra, 37–39
Friesen, Ingrid, R.D., L.D., 79–81
Frigge, Alice, 48–49

Graduate program, 60–61, 74, 76
Grimes, J. Frank, 12
Grocery store career, 1–14
Grocery store chain, 12
Groover, Riley, 34–36
A Guide to College Programs in Hospitality & Tourism, 84
The Guide to Cooking Schools—1996, 84

85

Index

Home economics teacher, 72
  profile of, 76–78
Host, 16
Hotel catering service, 46–47
Hotel chef, 23–25
Hotel work as training, 52
How to Open and Operate a Home-Based Catering Business, 56

Income and benefits, 3–4, 17–18, 31–32, 45–46, 59–60, 73–74
Independent Grocers Alliance (IGA), 12
Institutional foodservice, 29–42
Instructor, 75
Internship program, 14
Interviewing skills, 64

Job shadowing, 84
The Journal of the American Dietetic Association, 64

Kitchen worker, 16, 18, 30
Kroc, Ray, 26
Kroger, Barney, 12
The Kroger Grocery and Baking Company, 12

Lunch truck catering, 56

McDonald, Dick and Mac, 26
McDonald's restaurant, 26–27
Management, 3–7, 16–17, 19, 30, 47, 59–60
  profile of career, 9–11
  skills, 9–10, 20, 35
Market research, 12
Mass production in foodservice, 40
Master's degree, 60–61, 74, 76
Math skill, 5, 20
Mazi, Gabriella, 83
Melanson, Steve, 23–25
Mobile Industrial Caterers Association-International, 56
Mondavi, Robert, 83
Moscow Boys Choir, 22

National Education Association, 84
National Grocers Association, 14
National Restaurant Association, 28, 33, 42
Nation's Restaurant News, 28
Nutrition and health career, 57–70

O'Grady, Peter, 54
Organizational skill, 20, 47

Outdoor event, 53
Overton, Jill, 62–64
Owner-operator, 45–47, 60

Page, Karen, 56
Party planning, 46, 50
Prison foodservices, 34–36
Professor, 75
Public health, 61

Quiz for each career area, 13, 19, 41, 55, 69, 75

Ratner, Nancy, 76–78
Registered Dietitian (RD), 60
Research, 60
Research dietitian, 58–59
Restaurant career, 15–28
Restaurant catering service, 46–47
Restaurants & Institutions, 28
Restaurants USA, 28
Resume, 11, 14

Safety, Sanitation, and Food Protection, 42
Sales representative, 61
School foodservice, 30
Self-employment, 45–47, 60
Server, 16, 18, 30
Service clerk, 6
Service manager profile, 20–22
"Set Your Sites" (ADA video), 70
Smiley, Martha, R.D., 65–67
Sous chef, 23
Spiller, David, 6–8
Stock clerk, 3, 4, 6

Teaching, 71–84

University foodservice, 37–39
U.S. Department of Health, Education, and Welfare, 42

Vivaldo, Denise, 54, 56
Vocational school, 46, 72
Volunteering as training, 38, 48–49, 70, 80

Watson, Alicia, 20–22
Watson, Monty, 51–53
Wholesale network, 12
Work day description, 7, 36, 48–49, 72–73, 78

Yan, Martin, 83